High Anxieties!

by Sherrie Weaver

Getting the most out of Embarrassing Moments

Cover Design by Design Dynamics

Typography by MarketForce

Published by Great Quotations Publishing Co.,
Glendale Heights, IL

Library of Congress Catalog Card Number: 97-77640

ISBN 1-56245-335-1

Printed in U.S.A.

DEDICATION

To Jessica & Seth, who have given me more
than my fair share of embarrassing moments,
to Pat & Ringo, who have given me the
opportunity to embarrass myself in print,
rather than just in person, and to everyone who
has ever wanted to crawl red-faced into the next
parallel dimension to avoid those staring eyes.

Introduction:

If you are drawing breath on a regular basis,
you will eventually do something to embarrass yourself
or those around you (or both). A few folks manage to shake
off an embarrassing moment unscathed. But most of us,
myself included, wind up with these anxious moments sticking
to us like a 3 foot piece of toilet paper stuck to our shoe.

After spraining a wrist falling UPSTAIRS at my daughter's
football game, I realize that for some of those moments in life,
there is simply no recovery. Your best bet is to just relax,
read this book and laugh at somebody else.

The true definition of confidence
is walking out of a public restroom
without checking your fly.

A
N
X
I
E
T
Y

Just because a woman has a big belly,
it doesn't mean she's pregnant.
Better be sure before you ask,
"When are you due?"

It's bad enough to get
caught singing in the car.
It's worse when the
windows are down.

7

There is no way to look
'cool' with 2 feet of toilet paper
stuck to your shoe.

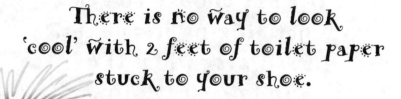

Always thank your hostess
for a fun evening.
If you had too much fun,
offer to pay the cleaning bill.

Have you ever left a long, intimate message on your beloved's answering machine, only to discover that your beloved doesn't have an answering machine?

ANXIETY

Then there was the gal who
finally overcame her fear
of public speaking, only to trip on
the stairs on her way up to the podium.

ANXIETY

ANXIETY

Ever discovered that your 9:00am telephone conference call was for a different time zone?

A crowded elevator is neither the time nor the place to discover that hard-boiled eggs and beer aren't "colon-friendly".

ANXIETY

"Uhm, honey, I'm at the gas station....
Did you by any chance
grab that $20 out of my wallet?"

"....Oh, and did you know that we're over our credit limit on the credit card?"

Great news! You found the button
that popped off your shirt.
Bad news, you didn't find it until
after the parent/teacher conference.

16

The only thing worse than
getting something stuck
between your teeth is forgetting
to put them in.

17

Nobody saw that patch of ice you slipped on. But the crowd of onlookers rated your fall as a 9.6, with a 3 point bonus for difficulty.

18

Perhaps the reason that Mr. Jones was looking so strangely at you throughout the entire conversation was that his name is Mr. Filmore.

After a heated protest and an usher's intervention, you discover that you really are in the wrong seats.

Always keep up with current events. The guy behind you in the check-out line may be the husband of the woman you've spent the last 20 minutes bad-mouthing.

You can honk all you want,
but if the turn arrow is red, the guy
in front of you probably won't move.

ANXIETY

ANXIETY

Not only did Junior repeat
those words you used last night,
but he did it at the top of
his voice, in church.

ANXIETY

23

ANXIETY

Falling asleep in a meeting is no big deal...unless you snore.

Faux Paux № 202: Size 9 dress,
size 13 body, size 3 dressing room.

ANXIETY

The reason your key won't unlock the door is that you're at the wrong apartment.

*Now where did I
park that stupid car?*

That joke you told was really funny.
Too bad those folks you told
it to didn't think so.

28

They had to stop the entire
ski lift to untangle you.
What if that was your
15 minutes of fame?

ANXIETY

If your horn gets stuck on
the highway, that's embarrassing.
If it gets stuck behind a biker gang,
that's life-threatening.

A
N
X
I
E
T
Y

A
N
X
I
E
T
Y

You really did leave your wallet
in your other pants.

The grocery order has been
totalled and bagged.
And your checkbook is still at home
on the table.

He's gained 40 pounds and lost all
his hair. And you still said,
"You look great."

This morning you walked to work, briefcase in hand, purse over your shoulder and dress tucked into your nylons. Next time, take the bus.

ANXIETY

Why is it that the drunker we get,
the smarter we think we are?

35

ANXIETY

Tomorrow, you will regret
both the 3 double whiskeys and
the Karaoke rendition of
'Amarillo By Morning'.
Tonight, your friends do.

He's a good dog
and he *loves* everybody.
Especially your neighbor's pant leg.

ANXIETY

The reason you didn't catch someone's name is that they didn't give it to you.

You've been putting groceries
into the cart all the
way down the aisle.
Except it's not your cart.

The reason that bounced check
displayed so prominently behind
the counter looks so familiar
is that it is yours.

You wrote the mortgage payment,
addressed and stamped the
envelope and stuck it in your
briefcase to mail.
Where it still remains.

A
N
X
I
E
T
Y

It's your brand new,
state-of-the-art car alarm.
And it's been going off for almost
an hour because you can't
figure out how to shut it off.

A
N
X
I
E
T
Y

You're a half hour early for your interview. You're dressed professionally and have an updated copy of your resume. However, your appointment was for yesterday.

The rule of computer usage says, "if your company has spent a great deal of money setting up the new system, you will be the one to foul it up."

The charming country
BBQ ribs place has quaint little
signs on the restroom doors.
One says 'Boars' and one says
'Gilts', and you have no idea
which one you are.

45

It was your best brown bag lunch yet.
BBQ chicken, chips, cookies.....
except it wasn't your lunch.
And whoever got your leftover
macaroni and cheese is gonna be hot.

The two of you have been
strolling through the mall having
a wonderful conversation.
Except she stopped 4 stores back
to look at a dress, and you didn't.

ANXIETY

You thought he paid for the meal,
and he thought you did.
Sure, they'll believe that.

The lock on the bathroom door
has never worked really well.
And now you're face to cheek with
someone who is just as startled
as you are.

Why did the little darling choose the longest grocery store line in history to ask where babies come from?

When did they change the
church service from 10:30 to 10:00?

51

Buffet-style restaurants are proof
that heartily-laden food trays are
best carried by trained professionals.

That little 'Push' sign on the door
was put there to confuse you.
Better try a good 'Pull' anyway.

When cutting anything, remember: sharp side down.

54

A N X I E T Y

You're been waiting for the elevator for 20 minutes. Wouldn't it help if you pushed the little arrow button?

55

Your husband used to love
a little pat on the tush.
He probably still does,
except the guy you just patted
isn't your husband.

Your keys are locked safely away.
Unfortunately, they are
dangling there in your ignition.

It's only been in all the papers
and on the television news.
So how come you missed the whole
"Daylight Savings Time" thing?

ANXIETY

ANXIETY

White skirt, red wine,
wobbly little glass....

ANXIETY

ANXIETY

The Secretary of State
is 3rd in line for the Presidency.
So why don't you know his name?

Someone just enthusiastically
greeted you by name.
You had a 10 minute conversation
and parted promising to stay in touch.
But you still have no earthly idea
who that person was.

ANXIETY

Those sunglasses,
the ones on top of your head,
are the ones you've spent
the last 20 minutes looking for.

Anyone can fall down stairs.
Falling up stairs, now that
takes a special talent.

You've been trying for 3 hours to remember the name of the guy who played the Skipper on "Gilligans Island". So when it finally comes to you, you just shout it right out.
(it was Alan Hale)

Your car is the fast food wrapper burial ground. And your boss needs a ride home.

A N X I E T Y

A N X I E T Y

A really full bladder and a really big sneeze.

A
N
X
I
E
T
Y

The two leather shoes you grabbed
this morning are lovely.
But they are from two different
pairs of shoes.

You bought the tickets, the soda and the popcorn and settled into your seat. But the movie you wanted to see is in the next theater.

Yes it is rather drafty in here.
It would probably be a bit warmer
if you'd zip up your fly.

The library book that you
swore vehemently you'd returned
just slid out from underneath
your front seat.

70

It occurs to you, that if you can hear
the neighbor's snoring
through his open bedroom window,
what can he hear through yours?

71

ANXIETY

No, there is nothing seriously
wrong with your car.
A little gas will fix it right up.

"There is a car in the parking lot
with it's lights on...."
and it's yours.

ANXIETY

Always keep a spare pair of panty hose.
Just don't keep them on
the leg of the slacks you're wearing.

If you spend 30 minutes in a restaurant putting down your boss, you should be very sure he isn't sitting in the next booth.

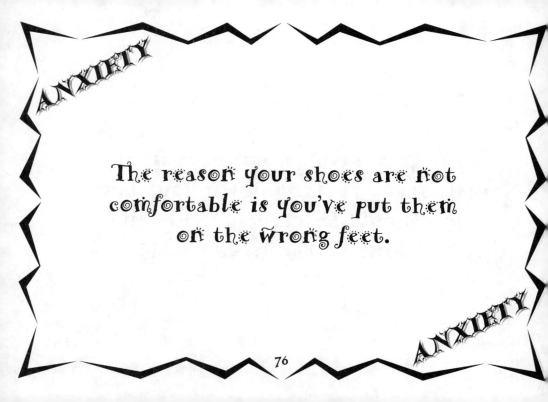

ANXIETY

The reason your shoes are not comfortable is you've put them on the wrong feet.

ANXIETY

76

About 3 hours after the meal,
you discover that at least
part of that spinach quiche you
had is still with you.
Between your front teeth.

Where will you be when you discover that too much Schnapps is not a good thing?

A
N
X
I
E
T
Y

You must have had a
really good time last night.
You just don't remember it.

A
N
X
I
E
T
Y

You're been on hold so long that
when they finally answer you,
you've forgotten why you called.

Never confuse the 'speaker'
button on your phone
with the 'hold' button.

Is that his wife,
or his college-aged daughter?

"I haven't seen you and Bob
around lately.."
"That's because he's in
Oahu with his mistress."

ANXIETY

You have to make the introductions.
So why can't you remember
the guy's name?

Everybody in your office said you were too old to in-line skate. So how are you going to explain the cast on your wrist?

ANXIETY

Your pantleg is caught firmly
in your bicycle chain. Ride on!

There is nothing wrong with
your copy machine that a little paper
in the tray wouldn't fix.

It's not broken, it's just unplugged.

You rear-ended the guy in front
of you because you were staring at
that blond on the corner.
The cop may understand,
but your wife won't.

Ever had to move your car to the other side of the pump because you forgot which side the tank is on?

"No, the Sexually Transmitted Disease Clinic is one door down."

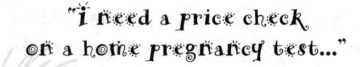

"I need a price check
on a home pregnancy test..."

92

Not only did you step in it,
but you've tracked it
all over the carpet.

ANXIETY

Boy, those hospital gowns really
do gap open at the back.

ANXIETY

ANXIETY

Give that child-proof medicine bottle
to any available 10 year old.
He'll get it open.

ANXIETY

ANXIETY

The clock on your car stereo has been flashing 12:00 since you bought it, because you can't figure out how to set it.

Remember when you took the
spare out of the trunk because
you needed more room?
Bet you wish you'd remembered to
put it back in.

The guy honking at you
isn't getting friendly.
He's trying to tell you that
you've shut your coat in the car door.

It's not acid rain washing down your windshield, it's the coffee cup you left on top of the car when you got in.

99

There is never a plunger in
a public restroom, even if one
is desperately needed.

Always wear white
if you're planning on
spilling something indelible.

You dyed your hair and it looks great.
All except that one streak
in the back that you missed.

A
N
X
I
E
T
Y

A
N
X
I
E
T
Y

Whose bright idea was it to put the buttons on the back of a dress?

Go head. Explain to your spouse
why your high school
nickname was 'Tubby'.

So, Mommy, why are the dogs
playing piggy back?

105

ANXIETY

You could have sworn that
the invitation said 'casual dress'.

ANXIETY

You didn't see the 'no smoking' signs.
Just the angry glares of
the *people* around you.

107

ANXIETY

You've got your team jacket,
your pennant and all the
beer money you need.
But the game tickets are still
on your dresser.

108

The turkey is stuffed,
marinated and has been in
the oven for 3 hours.
Except the oven isn't turned on.

You called in sick to work
so that you could go to the ball game.
How were you supposed to know
that the boss had season tickets,
and his wife was using them that day?

That's your best friend at that table, locked in a passionate embrace. Problem is, that ISN'T her husband.

You just told a series of riotously funny jokes about a certain religious denomination to a man who's wife is a member of that church. Start praying

112

Ever walked off without
waiting for your change?

Guess what?
The power company is correct,
you really haven't paid that bill.
You really are in the dark.

ANXIETY

It's bad enough when your
underwear rides up...
BUTT, when you get caught
digging it out....

ANXIETY

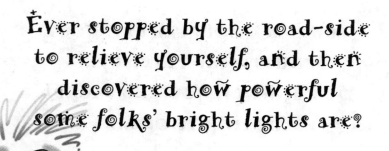

Ever stopped by the road-side to relieve yourself, and then discovered how powerful some folks' bright lights are?

It's ok to sing along with the radio.
But it helps to know the words.

The person you blamed your mistake on
wasn't in the office the day
the mistake was made.

118

Your shirt sleeves won't stay up,
but your bra straps do.

119

ANXIETY

You bowled a strike!
in the wrong lane.

You said you'd do it,
you meant to do it,
but forgot to do it.

ANXIETY

You spent all weekend finishing a project and left it on the kitchen table.

That stunning shade of pink on your underthings is proof that sorting your laundry is a good thing.

Those little yellow sticky notes
will adhere to almost anything.
Including the seat of your pants.

ANXIETY

is that your resume
in the office copier?

ANXIETY

A
N
X
I
E
T
Y

You forget to write down a check.
And every subsequent check
thereafter has helped you remember.

A
N
X
I
E
T
Y

You spend 25 minutes berating your teenager about the way she dresses. So she drags out your high school yearbooks.

127

A huge italian lunch complete
with lots of garlic bread.
So when 3 of your office mates
offer you a breath mint,
you probably shouldn't wonder why.

That dress is gorgeous.
But it's so tight you can't sit down.
Can you eat an entire
formal meal standing up?

For the rest of your career,
you will be known as 'the guy
who got drunk at the Christmas party
and ralfed on the boss.'

ANXIETY

A new silk tie, a bowl of chili and a dry cleaning bill.

ANXIETY

ANXIETY

Try explaining to the attending physician that you threw your back out doing the Limbo at a neighborhood BBQ.

You're the only one at the
entire table who still has
room for dessert.
And no one is surprised.

That car parked crooked across 2 spaces is yours. But it still looks straight to you.

You can't name the Vice President,
Secretary of State or
your own state Governor.
But you can name all seven dwarves
and six of the Mouseketeers.

Someone just told you that
you have a run in your nylons.
Only you're not wearing nylons.

136

The guy behind you is complaining
about the glare of light
off the top of your head.

A
N
X
I
E
T
Y

A
N
X
I
E
T
Y

You thought the invitation said 'Costume Party'.

138

A
N
X
I
E
T
Y

A
N
X
I
E
T
Y

The music has stopped,
but your booty is still shaking.

139

The officer wants to see
current proof of insurance.
Frankly, so do you.

High Anxiety Situation № 26:
A nasty allergy attack.
No tissues. A short sleeved shirt.

It's the most popular movie of all time.
Everybody is talking about it.
And you still haven't seen it.

ANXIETY

One size does not fit all.
Not even close.

ANXIETY

The one darn time you
answer your phone with
"Yo, baby, talk to me."
It's your boss.

Never drink 4 cups of coffee before a long staff meeting.

ANXIETY

Your car was towed because the cops assumed it was an abandoned vehicle.

Your wife and your secretary
sound very similar on the phone.
Mixing them up could make
either a very interesting day
or a very long night. Or both.

You thought you'd hung the phone up
before you began your tirade
against whoever was on the other end.

ANXIETY

This time, you were the bonehead who didn't look before you backed up.

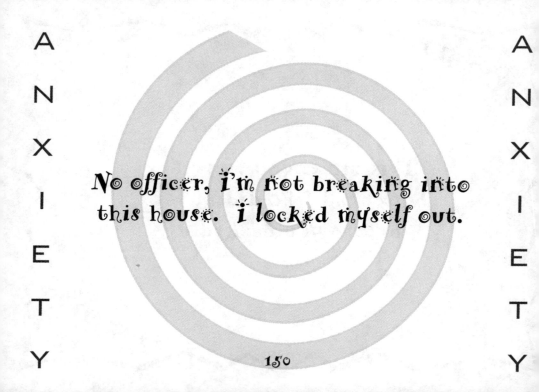

A
N
X
I
E
T
Y

A
N
X
I
E
T
Y

No officer, I'm not breaking into this house. I locked myself out.

A
N
X
I
E
T
Y

A
N
X
I
E
T
Y

It was a great movie.
Too bad you slept through it.

151

A long flight, a long nap
and a drool-soaked pillow.

It's a real crowded drive-thru,
and it took forever to be your turn.
As you pull up to the window,
you discover that you have no money.

You wrote a beautiful love letter.
But your love can't read
your handwriting.

ANXIETY

If you don't attend
the Symphony regularly,
it is probably a good idea not to
fill all the silences with applause.

ANXIETY

ANXIETY

That *full, flowing* skirt looked
real good in the house.
However, the wind wasn't blowing
so hard in your house.

Your sudden attack of motion sickness surprised both you and the guy next to you on the bus.

ANXIETY

Three days of pre-game bragging.
Loud boasting in the parking lot.
They lost anyway.

You have never forgotten
your first love. He, however,
has totally forgotten you.

That's your husband having
lunch over there.
Boy, is he surprised to see you...
and so is the woman he's with.

160

If those dryer fabric sheets prevent static cling, how come they stick to the back of your skirt?

A
N
X
I
E
T
Y

From a liquor store clerk:
"No, sir, i don't need to see your i.d."

A
N
X
I
E
T
Y

A
N
X
I
E
T
Y

A
N
X
I
E
T
Y

That lobster bisque looks wonderful.
Too bad he's allergic to seafood.

"No, I've never had chicken pox.
Why do you ask?"

"Your credit application is denied. But it was the funniest thing we've seen for some time, so thanks for trying.

i don't know my home phone number.
i never call myself there.

ANXIETY

ANXIETY

You dove deep into the pool.
Your suit didn't.

ANXIETY

Other Titles by Great Quotations

201 Best Things Ever Said
The ABC's of Parenting
African-American Wisdom
As A Cat Thinketh
Astrology for Cats
The Be-Attitudes
The Best of Friends
The Birthday Astrologer
Chicken Soup
Chocoholic Reasonettes
The Cornerstones of Success
Daddy & Me
Fantastic Father,
    Dependable Dad
For Mother, A Bouquet
    of Sentiments
Global Wisdom
Golden Years, Golden Words
Grandma, I Love You
Growing Up in Toyland
Happiness Is Found Along
    the Way
High Anxieties
Hollywords

Hooked on Golf
I Didn't Do It
Ignorance is Bliss
In Celebration of Women
Inspirations
Interior Design for Idiots
I'm Not Over the Hill
The Lemonade Handbook
Let's Talk Decorating
Life's Lessons
Life's Simple Pleasures
A Lifetime of Love
A Light Heart Lives Long
Midwest Wisdom
Mommy & Me
Mrs. Aesop's Fables
Mother, I Love You
Motivating Quotes
    for Motivated People
Mrs. Murphy's Laws
Mrs. Webster's Dictionary
My Daughter,
    My Special Friend
Only a Sister

The Other Species
Parenting 101
The Perfect Man
Reflections
Romantic Rhapsody
The Rose Mystique
The Secret Language of Men
The Secret Language
    of Women
The Secrets in Your Face
The Secrets in Your Name
Social Disgraces
Some Things Never Change
The Sports Page
Sports Widow
Stress or Sanity
A Teacher Is Better Than
    Two Books
TeenAge of Insanity
Thanks from the Heart
Things You'll Learn...
Wedding Wonders
Words From the Coach
Working Woman's World

GREAT QUOTATIONS PUBLISHING COMPANY
Glendale Heights, IL 60139
Phone (630) 582-2800 • Fax (630) 582-2813